Jacob was an old man, and a very happy man. He had twelve fine sons. He loved them all dearly, but Joseph was special.

Jacob was so fond of Joseph that he gave him a special coat. None of Jacob's other sons had such a beautiful coat. The brothers could see how much Jacob loved Joseph, and they were jealous.

Joseph also used to tell tales on his brothers. He told his father when they did not look after Jacob's flocks carefully enough. Joseph's brothers did not like him very much!

Joseph did not help matters by telling his brothers about two dreams he had. In the first dream Joseph imagined his brothers like sheaves of corn, all bowing down in front of him. In the second dream Joseph saw the sun, the moon and eleven stars, all bowing down to him.

His brothers were furious! "We're never
going to bow down to you," they said.

Then one day, the older brothers took their sheep and goats to graze a long way off. Jacob sent Joseph to see if they were all right. When the brothers saw Joseph in the distance, they said, "Here comes that dreamer!"

Then one brother said, "Let's kill him and throw him in a pit."

Joseph, the Dreamer

Pull out the stickers and these middle pages. Then read what to do next from the back page.

Now use your stickers!

This is what to do:

1. **Read the story right through so you know what happens.**
2. **Peel off each sticker carefully.**
3. **Use each sticker to complete the picture on the pages you have pulled out.**

More sticker books to collect!

There are 48 stories in this series, all with stickers. Collect all the stories and stick the completed middle pages round your bedroom wall.

"Yes, let's say a wild animal has killed him!" said another.

But when Reuben, the eldest brother, heard their plans, he said, "Throw him in the pit by all means, but do not kill him!" He meant to go back later to rescue Joseph. Then he went off to look after the sheep.

Some of the brothers stripped off Joseph's fine coat and threw him into a big hole in the ground. At first they just wanted to leave him there... but then they thought again. Some traders passed by on their way to Egypt, and the brothers decided they could sell Joseph instead.

They got a good price for him. Then, to try to cover things up, they dipped Joseph's coat in goat's blood, and took it back to Jacob their father.

They showed him the coat.

"He must have been killed by a wild animal," he cried. Jacob was heartbroken: the son he loved so much – dead!

Meanwhile, in Egypt, Joseph was working as a slave for a man called Potiphar, who was the captain of the king's guard. It wasn't much fun being a slave in a strange land instead of a rich man's son.

But Joseph worked hard. Potiphar knew he could trust him and soon he was in charge of everything in Potiphar's house. God was looking after him. But this was not the end of the story...